Seasons Siblings' Timeshare Tiff

San Francisco Whimsical Weather, Autumn 2016-Spring 2017

Deeann D. Mathews

ISBN 10: 1975818156
ISBN 13: 978-1975818159

First published in the United States by Deeann D. Mathews

Printed in the United States of America

To Gloria Sheppard, Helen Gill-Smith, Denise-Marie Standard Mitchell,
Evann Lyn Gastaldo Lutz, Anthony Mark Lamort, Paul Kiler,
and all my other social media friends who encouraged me
to get this story from the fun of posts into an actual book:
THANK YOU

Table of Contents

Meet the Seasons Siblings ……... 1

Prologue ……... 2

Day 1 4

Day 2 5

Day 3 part 1 6

Day 3 part 2 7

Day 4 8

Day 6 10

Day 7 12

Day 8 13

Day 9 part 1 16

Day 9 part 2 18

Day 10 20

Day 11 part 1 22

Day 11 part 2 25

Day 13 28

Day 15 part 1 29

Day 15 part 2 30

Day 16 31

Day 17 32

Epilogue 34

Meet the Seasons Family

Winter, the eldest Seasons brother, is the Northern Shepherd of the Turn of the year, and takes his responsibilities very seriously – his are grim tasks, and he has nor permits anyone else to have illusions about them. He is always cold and grand, logical, and no-nonsense. He can be brutal, as befits his reputation, but he also has a side to him which, if not warm, is milder and gentler. Ironically, he is closest to his sister Summer, who, like him, responsibly shepherds the turning of the years.

Spring, the elder Seasons sister, is flamboyant, passionate, and thus incredibly changeable. She thinks her elder brother Winter is too harsh, too cold, and basically a bore no matter what part of the year she meets him in – she loves flowers and warmth and the songs of birds and bees, and has no problem camping out in two hemispheres at once if she can get away with it. She loves taking San Francisco from her brother Autumn if he takes too long parting with sister Summer, and would turn October, November, and December into three extra months for herself – that is, if Winter would let her get away with December...

Summer, the younger Seasons sister, is the Southern Shepherdess of the Turn of the year. She loves all the things that Spring loves, and she ripens all the matters that Spring begins. Hers is that deep, inescapable heat that refines and matures all that has come before her. She is especially close to both Spring and Autumn, her fellow gardeners of the year, but has a warm spot in her vast, compassionate heart for her fellow year-shepherd Winter as well. She and Winter have in common their great depth of thought.

Autumn, the baby brother of the Seasons family, is the visual artist of the siblings. He loves the white of Winter, the green and pastels of Spring, the rainbow of colors of Summer, and also mixes with all that red and gold and silver hues that are his alone. He does this while he carries out his main task: completing the harvest Spring and Summer have labored to create, and preparing the plants and animals for the coming of Winter. The problem: in San Francisco, Spring just won't let him work in peace.

Prologue

In September, everything between the Seasons siblings was cool... or rather, warm...

Summer and Winter had a unique arrangement in San Francisco from June through August; because Summer was so hot as to melt the asphalt in some parts of the San Francisco Bay Area, their Creator had ordained that San Francisco and other parts of the coast of Northern California should have fog and be cool to provide relief. So, Winter, though he was in the Southern Hemisphere, blew misty kisses at his sister Summer while she was in San Francisco, until September.

In September, Summer at last showed her charms in San Francisco, and tended to overstay just a little bit into Autumn's time in the city. But Autumn did not mind that, for everywhere in the Northern Hemisphere, he and sister Summer always shared September, and sometimes he came early and – most often -- she stayed late. But that was all just fine, for both were deeply concerned with matters of the harvest and rejoicing in the bounty of the full work of the year -- even into early October, that was no problem.

But then came mid-October, and Autumn was confronted by the sister he didn't expect: Spring. She tipped in while her sister was departing in September, and suddenly everything that had bloomed in May started blooming all over again.

Spring did not interfere with Autumn's work with the trees, or the length of the days (for in that they were very similar anyhow), so he thought it was a fluke. Surely, they could share the city through October with no harm done.

But then October became November, then mid-November -- and then the last week of November came, and Spring was STILL playing in San Francisco. Autumn finally had enough, and brought the season's first significant storm on the night of November 22 and into the morning of November 23. But Spring was not going to give up that easily. The timeshare tiff thus began in earnest, and all four members of the Seasons family would get dragged into it before it was over...

Day 1, November 23

Said Spring to her brother Autumn: "Although I am impressed by your show of water force, I still am staying for Thanksgiving in San Francisco."

Said Autumn: "Very well, you sweetly impudent sister -- you dare reign in TWO hemispheres at once, which no season has EVER dared but you. But beware: our brother Winter will not be as kind about it as I have been. He will be here by this day in December!"

Said Spring: "He may and he may not... For I have stayed once or twice from September through June in recent years. I care not what the timeshare says on the calendar; if he is coming, let him come, but until then I may stay."

Said Autumn: "O saucy sister, rest assured: Winter IS coming!"

Said Spring: "That remains to be seen..."

Day 2, Thanksgiving, November 24:

No fighting this day in San Francisco; both Spring and Autumn gave thanks along with everyone in the city for their joint works of beauty. Autumn's heralds were in the sky, indeed, and the temperature was of Spring's warmth, but all was peace in the city... for one day, at least.

Day 3, November 25, part 1:

Spring and Autumn took a walk in San Francisco, including in that man-tended garden of God known as Golden Gate Park.

Said Autumn to Spring: "Look at this! You have the hollies and the rhododendrons disputing, the maples and the daisies in dispute!

Said Spring: "I know ... Isn't it lovely?"

Said Autumn: "Like San Francisco needs any more confusion!"

Said Spring: "But nothing is normal in San Francisco ever... isn't it nice to have such splendid confusion, if you insist on calling this that? I just call this splendid!"

Day 3, November 25, part 2:

Autumn sought counsel from his elder brother Winter about Spring overstaying in San Francisco. As one might expect, Winter's response was cool...

Said Winter: "Be contented, brother Autumn. Your time and mine will come... San Francisco is tilting away from the sun with the rest of the Northern Hemisphere, and our sister Spring already is not liking the chill of these longer nights."

Said Autumn: "She is resilient, rebounding by day-- will you not blow your breath upon her and encourage her to get moving to the Southern Hemisphere, where she belongs?"

Said Winter: "I rarely can blow her further than San Diego... she does like coastal California. But be content, brother. Tomorrow, I shall put a word in for you -- already, my heralds are in the sky."

Day 4, November 26:

Said Autumn to his elder brother Winter: "Are you kidding me? All these STILL out-of-place blossoms! And what about all those rainbows! Spring LOVES pastels-- now, she's going to want to stay in San Francisco even more! Some help you are, big brother!"

Said Winter, in a voice chilly with annoyance: "Cool it, baby brother-- and I mean that."

Autumn immediately calmed down. Of all the Seasons Siblings, Winter was the last one that you wanted to get out of line with.   He both ended and began every year in the Northern Hemisphere because he had the power and the will to keep everything in its proper order.

Said Winter: "Autumn, you are like your sultry sister Summer in temper, but you have not her power of mastery nor understanding. Do you not see the gain you shall have by continuing this day's work through Monday? The more days spent in cold rain, the cooler the nights as well, and the days grow too short for Spring's comfortable warmth to overcome the cumulative chill of many such days."

Said Autumn: "Oh, but a nice cold snap would solve it all!"

Said Winter: "You think you are having trouble now -- but suppose what would happen to your beloved maples and cherries and other trees if I did what you are asking -- in NOVEMBER!"

Said Autumn: "Well... I suppose not, brother."

Said Winter: "Quite rightly you suppose not! But if you will do what I have shown you today consistently, you will find the beginning of December much more to your liking."

Meanwhile, Spring, knowing that her cooler brothers were plotting, kept her own council.

"They think they will drive me from this city with a little rain... this city that loves me! Not hardly, gentlemen, not hardly, not yet!"

Weeping, Spring departed the city of San Francisco for the weekend, and Autumn thought he would now have all things as they should be, according to the calendar. Little did he know: the timeshare tiff was just beginning...

10

Day 6, November 28:

Seeing that Autumn had matters in hand in San Francisco -- however temporarily-- Winter, who as yet had no duties in San Francisco, decided to go talk with his sister who was likewise in waiting: Summer. Although they were as different as hot and cold or day and night, Winter enjoyed the perspectives of his sister, for she, like him, was masterful in her time, and steady of habit.

Sister Summer looked up in her perennial estates near the Equator, in surprise at a cool breeze on her. It was Winter, arriving, with his usual refreshing welcome in such climes.

Said Summer: "Beloved Winter – so far south?"

Said Winter: "Doubtless Spring has told you of her mischief in San Francisco."

Said Summer: "Yes, she was very upset with how you helped Autumn take over. But I told she ought to be content here, her proper place."

Said Winter: "I am pleased you were firm with her. Our brother was very put out, so much so he forgot himself with ME, so you know he is put out."

Said Summer: "Of course he is. Autumn is a visual artist, with that same temperament. Now Spring is a renaissance artist indeed -- all that fresh green with every cheery color playing against it, while the symphony of bird song and buzzing insects plays along. But whoever painted with green, and red, and gold, and orange, and brown as Autumn does in his time?"

Said Winter: "No one. It is indeed our Creator's special grant to him."

Said Summer: "Consider yet further, my brother. My equatorial estates are always mine. The poles, and the highest peaks are ever yours. Spring ever has the subtropics-- and she will have the entire earth in the coming times of refreshment our Creator shall yet bring upon the earth."

Summer paused a moment to let her brother consider all that she had said thus far. She was the Southern Shepherdess of the Turn, and so knew things even as her brother the Northern Shepherd knew things. She and Winter had the heavy conversations about the order of the universe, the year's weather orders, and the career of the Seasons siblings in light of time and eternity.   That went with being year-shepherds. So also did the deep concern for their more changeable siblings.

Said Summer: "But, Autumn, in eternity and now -- to whence can he go, brother Winter, when he is robbed of time and season? He is put out indeed!"

Said Winter: "That is DEEP, my sister Summer. No one gives you credit for it, but while humans bask and play, you are clearly thinking all the time. I so enjoy spending time with you."

Said Summer: "Be careful, brother. Show too much love and you'll ruin your cold reputation."

But Winter, once in his mild mood, was not easily put out of it. He smiled, almost warmly.

Said Winter: "I remember the day trips you spent in San Francisco in November 2015. Autumn and I enjoyed having you, those few days."

Said Summer: "Yes, that was fun, changing the season every two days through November. But I noticed you kept a cold wind blowing around every northern corner, and of course I understood your point. December was and is near, and we must assert ourselves indeed, you in the north of the world, me in the south. But I look forward to your foggy greeting in San Francisco, when I come north in June."

Said Winter: "You know that I shall blow misty kisses at you and the city all the while you are there. Until then, my sister!"

Said Summer: "Until then, my brother!"

Day 7, November 29:

Autumn, upon seeing that Spring had entrenched herself again in San Francisco, lost his temper and decided to get creative in the sky to get his message across...

Said Autumn to his sister Spring: "Notice the direction the clouds are pointing-- go THAT WAY, sister, THAT WAY!"

Said Spring: "Thank you for the pointer, kind brother. Since your sign points NORTHWEST instead of SOUTH or SOUTHEAST, I think I will go today and bring my charms to the Marin Headlands and other parts of coastal California. You're SO generous, brother Autumn! But rest assured; after I have made my visits, I'm coming right back here to my beloved city by the bay!"

Autumn looked up and realized his mistake.

Said Autumn: "AAAAAAAAAAAAGH!"

Day 8, Wednesday, November 30:

Autumn, still enraged by his sister Spring's return, summoned more clouds from the south, and brought on a surprise storm...

But while the rain indeed changed the aspect of the city, Spring blew her warm breath upon the storm and changed it to more like the storms of May, with breaks of sun and clouds like scoops of cotton candy on the sky...

Said Spring: "How nice of you to water my flowers, brother Autumn!"

Autumn held his peace, but went angry to his elder brother Winter.

Said Winter: "Today is the last day of November. I will speak with Spring tomorrow."

Said Autumn: "Tomorrow? Tomorrow? There's always tomorrow, eh -- when you could just blow her out of here?"

One cold look and thunderous rumble from Winter put an end to Autumn's burst of temper.

"I SAID, I WILL SPEAK WITH HER TOMORROW, AUTUMN."

Winter held his icy silence for a long minute, and then spoke more gently.

"Remember, brother: the treasures of the snow and hail, of stormy wind and frost, are not mine to use capriciously. I am merely the steward of the great cold, awaiting our Creator's will. I do not have His permission to blow upon November here this year. Besides, you would have things in hand if you had followed my advice about cold, steady rain. Your inconsistency is to blame for your sister's return."

Autumn was not pleased with that response, but he dared not talk back to his brother Winter a second time. He could only hope his brother would be as firm with his sister the next day...

Day 9, December 1, part 1:

The first day of December dawned as lovely as it possibly could, bright and calm and warm -- warm for December, anyhow, owing to the presence of Spring. San Francisco was a masterpiece of the Creator's lavish handiwork, the colors and gifts of Spring, Summer and Autumn all in display at once.

However, as Spring exulted in three seasons of glory at once, she noticed the first stirrings of a wind... it was not yet cold in the shade, but around shady corners that morning, there were whispers of polar airs. And that could only mean one thing. Mr. Cold-Trouble-in-Paradise, himself, was coming. Above the balmy palm trees, clouds of ice crystals appeared, until the condensation of ice seemed to fill the whole sky...

... and there Winter stood in San Francisco, in his cold grandeur, to confront his sister, Spring.

Said Spring: "What are you doing here?"

Said Winter, icily: "I am surveying what I shall shortly possess. How dare you ask, given that it is not March, April, May, or June?"

Said Spring: "I ask because I am welcomed here, in this lovely city, unlike you! Who would not have me, beautiful to the eyes and senses, at all months of the year?"

Said Winter: "The One Who said summer and winter, seedtime and harvest shall remain as long as the earth endures. Indeed, you are beautiful, sister Spring, and there is none lovelier..."

Winter paused a moment for emphasis, allowing his proud, flamboyant sister to savor his compliment before he said the rest: "But you are showing your vanity in San Francisco -- all the more reason for you to depart this Vanity Fair of the Pacific, for you and it encourage each other's special failings."

Said Spring: "Can you make me leave, for all your harsh talk? And if you could, the city would mourn! Who wants all your gray dripping, your bitter wind, your bare trees and sad limp greenery?"

Said Winter: "Every plant and piece of ground that needs rest after a year of labor – labor made longer by your playing here – welcomes me. As for harsh talk, try this: when my work is before me, do you think the opinion of this city – or yours -- is of any consequence to me?"

And in his voice was the depth of the thunder, the roar of the tempest, and stillness of cold death, all rolled into one. Spring was stunned silent..

"Hear me well, sister. If the poppies and the roses and the daisies mean more to you than mere playthings, you will let your brother serve his purpose in preparing them for rest. For on December 21, your playthings become MINE, and I will not spare them!"

Winter touched six of seven hydrangeas blooming nearby. They instantly died, leaving only one alive.

Said Winter: "Beware, sister! You have played in San Francisco right into December, but know this: I am NOT playing with you."

And then the sky cleared; Winter had departed. But he had left such a pool of cold air behind him that in the middle of the sunny day, Autumn was able to assert command! At least, for that day...

Day 9, December 1, part 2:

Spring retired to the Southern Hemisphere weeping violently... as one might expect, she was a sensitive soul with warm feelings, and Winter had not spared those feelings at all. But, on returning to her proper hemisphere, Spring found her younger sister Summer, waiting with open and comforting arms.

The Southern Shepherdess of the Turn loved her flamboyant elder sister deeply, and, since it was December 1, she too put forth her early grandeur, and drove off all the cold still lingering on Spring from Winter's early blast.

Said Spring: "Please don't say I told you so!"

Said Summer: "I would never do that to you."

No indeed... for Spring too was powerful, and if she really became angry, she had tornadoes to throw at both her near siblings! But, she most often cried herself out, and Summer was her usual comforter... Summer, younger, and yet so wise.

Said Summer: "Everything needs a rest, darling sister. The days are short, the nights are long and cold, and the ground chilled in the north... our beloved flowers are setting seed to be eaten only. But in March, sister, and April and May and June, then they shall have life, for the time will be yours. Stay here with me, for here, December is mine and yours to share in beauty, warmth, and love!"

Said Spring: "Well, I'm definitely not going back up there today..."

But she thought, "Winter cannot do this to me! I'm not yet done in San Francisco -- NOT YET!"

Meanwhile, Autumn went to his brother Winter in humility and gratitude.

Said Autumn: "Thank you, brother. That was truly awesome, and right on time!"

Said Winter: "All things in their time, Autumn. Owing to San Francisco's maritime climate and lawless ways, it can and does flout you -- but usually, not US. December is ours in the Northern Hemisphere, and if you can just keep that in mind and act accordingly, you will have less trouble in the next three weeks."

Said Autumn: "Do you think Spring will try to come back?"

Said Winter: "She will be back tomorrow if you don't watch what you are doing. But it is December now... if you need my help, I am near."

And Autumn looked up and saw the icy fringe of Winter's robe, brilliant upon the sunny sky, and he too was comforted.

Day 10, December 2:

On December 2, Autumn rose early and began using that cold air pool his brother Winter had left him and began whipping the leaves from the trees... for the first time in San Francisco, that year, it SOUNDED like Fall!

But to his dismay, some already-bare plum trees put forth a few buds in the wind... the day had grown warm and the true cold had been knocked out of the breeze. Spring had returned, and seized the day!

Autumn cried out: "Brother Winter!"

Winter at once flipped the fringe of his icy robe toward San Francisco; fresh cold air came rushing from the north! But he could only balance the conditions; the day still became very warm at moments because of the presence of Summer herself, coming in compassion to reason with her sister. And so, upon this one day, all four seasons could be felt in San Francisco.

Said Summer: "The city is lovely, sister, but remember... we have every city of the Southern Hemisphere in loveliness."

Said Spring: "I have my reasons! I have my reasons -- look at them, Summer! Why should their fresh beauty be frozen out! NO!"

Said Summer: "You are not being fair, sister, to our brothers."

Said Spring: "Life isn't fair! They can have San Francisco when they can hold it -- not before!"

Autumn whipped around, a thousand leaves whipping from a dozen trees as he did so.

Said Autumn: "Oh, so you want a trial of strength, eh?"

But the Northern Shepherd of the Turn intervened with all his cold logic.

Said Winter: "No, brother. First of all, there is no need to be an 67-time loser. 66 days of getting whipped by your sisters since September 21 should suffice you."

(Summer tried hard not to laugh, and quickly nudged her sister Spring to keep her from laughing.)

Said Winter: "Secondly, brother, Summer is here now. She will not permit you to blow Spring out roughly. I could insist, of course, but the city is completely unprepared for such a contest of wills between myself and equally mighty Summer. So, no, Autumn. Do not engage with our sisters; keep working with the trees and your other business, and I will make sure our sisters don't get too comfortable. It is December in the North, and I will remind them of where they are."

Day 11, December 3, part 1:

Said Summer to her sister Spring: "You are right; the city is beautiful, but it is transitioning, Spring, transitioning to the beauty of Winter, even beyond Autumn."

Spring stopped with her flowers for a moment, and looked up...

Said Spring: "Well, I have never looked at his work from this side... there is a certain grandeur and splendor to it."

Said Summer: "It is high, hard splendor, and indeed not as personable as ours, and not gentle. There is something frightening about our brother, indeed, something inimical to small and fragile things."

Spring looked again at her flowers, and nodded.

Said Summer: "That is why our Creator set it forth that he should only have three months, and that the temperate climates should then have us to enjoy after Winter has rested the plants and provided most of the water for the year. And then He provides Autumn to prepare the flowers and the trees to rest... for indeed how cruel would it be to give the small, lovely flowers from us into Winter's time, without Autumn's time for them to wind to a close of their work?"

Said Summer: "There is a reason for every time and season, in its place. Neither Winter nor Autumn hate the flowers we love, Spring... they just have a different function with them, and in the Northern Hemisphere, it is Autumn's time to put them to rest so that Winter may do his work without hurting them."

Said Spring: "When you say it, it makes more sense."

Said Summer: "I'm glad you recognize that, but you must do something with the recognition. The Southern Hemisphere is swooning with love for you and us, in the right time, and your flowers there will have a happy ending, for they will come to me and become fruit. Here... well, you know Winter cannot manage any fruit but citrus. Unlike his three younger siblings, our eldest brother is no gardener!"

Spring smiled through her tears, and no season was lovelier than she when she did that.

Said Spring: "No, he is no gardener at all... but he waters and weeds better than anyone."

Said Summer: "So why put him in a position he simply has no aptitude for and will not even attempt to get into? NOBODY stays in his lane and insists that everybody else stay in theirs like Winter!"

Said Spring: "Why can't he just be flexible?"

Said Summer: "You and Autumn are the flexible ones. Winter and I are respected for our stability, but because he is stable, he is not likely to be flexible with the consequences if ..."

Spring heaved a sigh, and Autumn, seeing her sadness, softened his aspect. He said nothing, giving Spring the day to think on what she should do next. He was following the silent cue of his colder brother, who drew his ice flames in the sky, but withheld his cold breath upon his sisters as they conversed.

For Winter knew Spring better than anyone, and in her time he rejoiced in her more than any other. He would not tolerate her out-of-season tricks, but he loved her, and grieved to think upon what would occur should she still be trying to garden in San Francisco on one of his heavy January or February work days. Winter knew, of course, that Summer's warm reasoning of course would likely better than his cold, harsh logic on Spring... he had made his point, and now withheld his cold so Summer could complete the purpose of her visit.

Maybe. Spring, flamboyant and changeable, could be reasonable one day and totally out of control the next. She was the inventor of the tornado; enough said. Winter knew he had to be prepared for all eventualities.

Day 11, December 3, part 2:

Sunset and evening came, and then night, and in December, a clear calm day meant a clear, calm and very cold night. Thus, the warm sisters Spring and Summer preferred to be early to bed... but Spring looked up and saw ice crystals frosting the face of the sky, and making the stars and moon misty.

Said Spring: "As if it were not cold enough already in this spot..."

Sure enough, Winter arrived to chat... hardly a fireside chat, of course, but he was in his mildest aspect.

Said Winter: "Good evening, sisters."

Spring fixed her mouth like she was going to say something smart, but Summer nudged her first, and they both greeted their elder brother.

Said Winter: "I have not come to chide with either of you; my position is clear. I have come to ask a question of you, sister Spring."

Sister Spring was not quite over their last conversation.

Said Spring: "Whaddya want, you cold flower-killing brute! Some brother you are!"

Said Summer: "Spring, do you dare disrespect the Northern Shepherd of the Turn?"

Said Winter: "It is of no consequence. It actually illustrates the purpose of my question. What exactly is so special about San Francisco that you would risk getting on the truly rough side of me, Spring?"

Said Spring, in a voice that recalled the thunder of her mighty supercell storms: "If you have to ask, you'll never understand."

Said Winter: "That's just it, Spring. I don't. I was not created to be like you."

Winter rose to move about as he spoke, but checked himself. No need to start a winter storm out of a clear night. He settled back down, and the air around him sank and deepened in cold.

Said Winter: "I have the heaviest stewardship of all, my sisters. For our Creator is the Alpha and the Omega, the Beginning and the End. And He in His infinite wisdom has set me, in an infinitesimal way, as a mirror: I am an end, and a beginning. With me, one year ends and another begins. Through me, those things not strong enough or meant to live perennially die, so that other plants and animals may feed and be fertilized and have room for when you come, Spring. Through me, the ground and trees rest, so they may wake refreshed.

"Through me, my sisters, blaspheming men in northern climes have occasion to remember: they who think themselves equal with God fear my terrors, and thus remember that they are only men. They remember that they too are but small, weak creatures in my resistless grip, and how much smaller still they are in the hand of my Creator, the rough side of Whom they do even better to avoid by finding refuge in the Son, Whose birth they celebrate in a figure while I am abroad. But it is hardly a baby Who commands me blow harsh, deadly reality into the New Year in the North!

"For I am also the figure of Death: cold, immobilizing, resistless... not final to those creatures that have life within them to wake again in a new year, but final to the last degree of finality to those that do not. And so, to northern men I carry the same dread reminder: Death comes, and those who have been granted life in the Son will rise again to eternal life. Those who have not life in the Son will not have life again, but eternal death."

Said Spring: "You do all that?"

Said Winter, mildly: "Now do you understand why I can't tend your flowers? And, since you know and love this city so much: do you not think it has just a few men who need my kind of reminder?"

Winter smiled, and frost crystals glittered around him like a shower of diamonds.

Said Winter: "Think about it this weekend, and good night."

He departed, and Summer dispelled most of the cold pool he left in his wake.

Said Spring: "Say, sister, if he's the figure of Death in these parts..."

Summer sighed, and said, "What time of year is it when preachers say, 'If you think it's hot now, don't you mess around and end up in --?"

Said Spring: "Got it. And Autumn?"

Said Summer: "He reminds man that all who live must complete their work and may rejoice in that which is good from their labors, but all the while, timely prepare, for Death is coming."

Said Spring: "But what about...?"

Said Summer: "And this is the part that makes our brothers think you are crazy, fussing over some daisies in December in San Francisco. Don't you know you are a portrait of renewed life after death, warm after cold, pleasant waking after troubled sleep, a season that ever passes into even fuller life?"

Said Spring: "No... I think more about the daisies."

Said Summer: "A lot of people are like you: eternity at hand, and they are focused on whatever their daisies are. But in you, it is all right... you'll catch that when you get your assignment in the new earth our Creator will make. Night night, sis."

Day 13, December 5:

In peace and quietness, Autumn reigned though Spring remained in San Francisco for two days, through Winter's advice to him and his quiet help: he moved his robe of ice crystals even more thickly over the sky, and left his robe there, allowing Autumn to hang his silver mists upon them. Summer had not yet left watching over her sister, so the temperature could not get too cold, but with Winter above, Summer below, and neither in possession, who could reign but Autumn, who was indeed in his rightful place?

For two nights, Autumn finally was able to bring his sweet, heavy dew to the city, and Spring decided to see how he would treat her beloved blooms and tender herbs if she left him alone. Everywhere, he lay his silvery loveliness, and all was well. The scenes reminded her of something she had seen before. As she paused by some orchids, brother Autumn eased over beside her.

Said Autumn, softly: "I never can look at any flower at this time of year without thinking of how the city, and all of us Seasons, rejoiced when Winter finally relaxed his grip and let the frost again be dew... and when your warm breath over many days stirred these plants to blooming life. And now..."

Said Spring: "And now with your cool breath, you want to put them back to sleep in the dew, before Winter wraps them in his blanket of frost."

Gently, Winter and Summer came and stood behind them and quoted, their voices a harmony of the highest highs and deepest lows of all Creation: "To everything there is a season, and a time to every purpose under heaven."

Autumn reached out to his sister Spring.

"I know you love San Francisco, and so do I... Will you trust me? Please?"

Day 15, December 7, Part 1:

Spring stood another day and another night, observing the beauty of her brother Autumn's idea of a sunny day. His bright coolness was not unfriendly to the city's many flowers, only encouraging their parent plants: "Save the rest: Spring will return with Summer next year, I promise!" There was fruit to be seen too, as Autumn had not forgotten his bounty even as he encouraged the trees also to rest.

Then had come night, deep and cold... In December, Autumn began to approach his brother Winter in such depths, but his was the cold that made sleep agreeable to everyone.
The new day, December 7, had dawned silver once again... the chief beauty of Autumn in San Francisco above, with the last colorful show of flowers, fruit, and trees below.

Said Spring: "It is enough. I am ready now."

She embraced her brother warmly, and went with her sister Summer to the Southern Hemisphere.

Brother Winter withheld a deep, cold sigh of relief... for he knew his baby brother. It was a cold victory indeed for Autumn, with little joy. He had not vanquished an enemy, but sent away a friend in his lovely sister. Of course it had to be done; Winter had no sentiments about that fact. But he knew: Autumn, sensitive artist type that he was, was actually heartbroken for missing Spring, already.

So Winter withheld his sigh of relief, for Autumn went about his business in sorrow, and some time that day he would weep. San Francisco was hardly ready for snow, after all, so Winter slowly breathed out his cooling vapors, and awaited the inevitable...

Day 15, December 7, part 2:

Autumn reigned in silver splendor;
Every hue cried "Victory!"
But everywhere the willows wept,
So did he.

San Francisco had submitted;
Spring had gone, as all could see,
But everywhere the willows wept,
So did Autumn; so did he.

Day 16, December 8

For six hours, and for twelve, for eighteen and even for twenty-four, Autumn could not withhold his sorrow, but wept passionately for missing his sister Spring. Rain and leaves came down in abundance, across the city. The earth of San Francisco also responded, sending up great clouds of tulle fog to meet Autumn's silver robe... as if to hide from each other the extent of the other's sorrow.

And yet, even in his grief, Autumn was ever the careful gardener and artist, and he spread his silver to the ground in drops of silver and silver-cast diamonds. And everywhere he saw a reminder of his sister Spring, he tearfully lavished it, so that it had the full of her beauty and his as well.

Brother Winter knew he was no comforter, and so held his peace. Even as Autumn's passion warmed the day so much that Spring might be tempted to return if the warmth persisted, Winter withheld his cold breath, out of respect for his brother's feelings.

As the day came to a close, Autumn, still in tears, spoke to his elder brother.

"What you lack in warmth you make up in wisdom, my brother Winter. The best comfort is sometimes what is not said or done when it is not necessary to say or do anything but be near. Thank you."

Said Winter: "You're welcome, brother Autumn. I am near for you, always."

After 36 hours of weeping, Autumn was able to come to himself in peace. Ironically, it was as warm as any day on which his sister Spring had played in the city just a week before, but the storm of his grief had so altered the local climate that no, she surely could not return. The city was not for her; it was his. So, Autumn dispersed the tulle fog, and showed himself in all his glory. It was done; all the Seasons siblings were in their rightful place, and he reigned in San Francisco, as was fit.

Winter was not due in San Francisco to reign yet, so he prepared to depart.

Said Winter: "Well done, brother Autumn. Be of good courage, and make good use of the next twelve days. I do not object to you remaining with me for the rest of December either, provided the orders for the end of 2016 and the beginning of 2017 permit it."

Said Autumn: "I may need the extra time; I am behind in terms of the tender herbs, flowering plants, and some flowering trees. But you know I enjoy hanging out with you anyway, big brother."

Said Winter, mildly: "You are always welcome, so long as you don't try any tricks with me in April."

Said Autumn: "Who, me? Oh, no. I need a full palette to work with, and April doesn't have it. But speaking of April... Is Spring going to be back in San Francisco on time, or early?"

Said Winter: "The book of the weather in 2017 has not been opened to me yet, but even if it were, what is in it would neither be yours to know nor mine to tell you. Of the times and seasons, only the Creator may know, and those to Whom He will reveal them."

Said Autumn: "Oh, come on, bro! It's December 9! You have to know something by now!"

Said Winter: "All right. Come close to me, brother; this is not for others' ears."

Autumn drew near to his brother, and, in a whisper as soft and cold as snow, there came the secret...

Said Winter: "It will be colder in January than it is now."

The clouds split overhead at Autumn's uproarious laughter.

Said Autumn: "I should have known you were messing with me!"

Winter smiled, and with that, went to his estates in Antarctica -- in the Southern Hemisphere. As he passed through Spring's rightful December dominion, he spoke to her:"Your brother and I will welcome you in San Francisco once again, at the proper time. Until then, my sister, farewell."

In spite of herself, Spring smiled. Winter was showing his mild side, the side she knew well and loved. But Spring would ever be Spring: flamboyant and capricious, and especially concerning the most flamboyant and capricious city in the Northern Hemisphere.

Said Spring: "Farewell, brother Winter, but don't get too comfortable in San Francisco. I WILL be back-- in February if you don't look sharp. January if you turn your back! In fact --."

Said Summer her sister: "Spring, give it a rest!"

Spring settled down in the Southern Hemisphere, where she had plenty of work to do. But she began planning her magnificent return to San Francisco, her beloved city. After all, March was four months away, and indeed, she would find her way back early if she could. For certainly she would dare...

THE END (but not really...)

Epilogue: Winter 2016-2017 vs. Drought...

Drought, that monster who has Ruin and Famine as its spawn and Death as its friend, will not itself die until the Creator renews the earth. So, with that knowledge, the beast had settled securely in California before 2017. But, the un-sentient, uncaring beast knew not that Winter, the Northern Shepherd of the Turn, also loved California, and the city of San Francisco.

Winter was merely awaiting the proper time to deal with Drought. He had no illusions that he could kill it; of all the seasons, the Northern Shepherd of the Turn was least given to delusions of grandeur. On the other hand, he knew the extent of his own power, and when he saw what was written in the Book of the Year for 2017, he smiled, put on his war robes (heavy robes, with abundant moisture and jet stream power knitted right in), unsheathed his rain-shaft sword, and set forth.

Through the end of December, through January, February, and half of March, Winter and Drought did terrible battle in California. Spring and Autumn were both very glad they had left San Francisco by then, for it was no fun for any of the Californians. Hillsides collapsed. Roads washed out. Floods raged. Towns were cut off, one from another. People actually died. Winter noted this with great gravity. But he had his orders, and he was going to carry them out, come what may.

In March, Drought had taken all it could stand, and fled before the rain curtains and dripping sword of Winter. In one season, Winter had undone Drought's withholding of water in such a way that Drought could no longer remain, save in the desert parts of California which were its right domain. There it withdrew to lick its wounds, and Winter, his work done, sheathed his mighty sword. He ended his reign in slowly warming quiet, for now, just now, it was time for Spring's rightful return...

… And The Return of Spring, March 20, 2017

Spring came in her rightful time to San Francisco to reign in soft showers, with all the tokens of her presence now in their timely and rightful glory. But she also came in wonderment. For the first time in six years, Drought, that horrid beast, had been driven from the city and the state -- and, oh, what glories that would mean for Spring, Summer, and Autumn, in their times!

Winter, the Northern Shepherd of the Turn, stood in San Francisco to say goodbye to his sister. His grim aspect was much softened; his work was done.

Said Winter: "Farewell, sweet sister. I am going to my Arctic estates until May, so I will not be far. If you have any need, call for me and I will come instantly to your aid."

Spring looked all her dutiful elder brother had prepared for his siblings, and wrapped her arms around him.

Said Spring: "Oh, dear brother, I love you! You have driven Drought out and given us all refreshing and hope of greater joys than we have had in years! Thank you, my brother-- thank you so much!"

Said Winter: "I have only done that which was my duty to do... and also my pleasure, Spring. Be beautiful in your time, beloved sister, for it is your time! Farewell!"

Spring kissed her brother on his high, cold forehead, and the warmth of her kiss floated him out of San Francisco into the jet stream, from which he flew to the North Pole, well-pleased. All was well, and the Seasons Siblings Timeshare Tiff was over.

Until October comes again, at least...

The End

(almost)

If You Have Enjoyed This Book...

Hello from the author, Deeann D. Mathews – thank you for reading Seasons Siblings Timeshare Tiff! I'd appreciate it so much if you would do just one more thing: if you have enjoyed this book, please leave a review if you purchased it on Amazon, GoRead, or wherever else you may have found it. Thank you, and thanks again for reading!

www.ingramcontent.com/pod-product-compliance
Lightning Source LLC
Chambersburg PA
CBHW040148240726
48664CB00002B/632